Geeks Guide to Interviews:
15 Critical Items for the Technical Type

Simple Steps to Win the
Technical Interview

Tim Goldstein

Disclaimer:

Tim Goldstein is neither a professional licensed therapist nor a licensed medical doctor. Tim draws on his vast experience living life both diagnosed and undiagnosed with Aspeger's as well as his extensive business and technical backgrounds. While Tim may give his interpretation of defined medical conditions and may use medical terms in non-medical ways, he is not giving any professional of medical advice. If you are in doubt, seek a qualified provider specializing in Aspegergers.

Tim Goldstein can be contacted through his website

www.TimGoldstein.com

Get more Geeks Guide to Interviews resources at:
https://www.TimGoldstein.com/p/GGtI

Published by:
Wiser Publishing
PO Box 621294
Littleton, CO 80162

ISBN: 1542595215
ISBN-13: 978-1542595216

DEDICATION

I dedicate this book to my amazing wife Karen. She has been through all the ups and downs you can have in 32 years of marriage to a hypomanic Aspie. She has always been my most avid supporter. Karen has coped and tolerated me as we work at learning to better deal with the neurotypical versus Asperger's communication barrier. Most of all, she has encouraged me and kept me looking forward. Especially on those days when the only movement seemed to be backwards. Thank you Karen for all the love, caring, sacrifice, and even kicks in the butt when needed. I love you.

CONTENTS

Tim Goldstein

ACKNOWLEDGMENTS

The list of people that helped me make this book a reality is extensive. First is our daughter Joanna. She is my #2 biggest supporter and has always encouraged and supported me, even when she couldn't understand me. She give me a more balanced perspective than my Aspie mind creates and advices me when I am at the limits of my ability to cope. She is also my media and communication consultant without whom I would be drowning.

A big thank you goes out to my mother. While we have always had an unconventional parent child relationship, Ma taught me to not just dream, but to put action behind those dreams and see where they go. Without this spirit of adventure I would not be where I am.

Roger Love changed my life and was a key player in saving my marriage. I thought I was studying with him to improve my voice. Instead, Roger reached in and pulled out the better me which he saw hidden inside.

Bo Eason has influenced me in ways that are hard to explain. He taught me I have the strength to stand up to anyone. He showed me the struggle is my strength and to honor it as the path to improvement.

Mel Abraham helped with and taught me many things, especially about frameworks. Mel's unique approach to making the complex simple is amazing, just like Mel.

Thanks to Brendon Burchard. He got me motivated to head down this path then taught me the initial steps. He gave me the vision of what is possible and introduced me to Roger, Bo, Mel, and a number of others who helped me learn not just skills, but belief in myself.

Damien Boudreaux is both an angel from heaven and a friend. Damien's creative "I am" and "We are" exercises along with his wise council was another key to saving our marriage and letting both Karen and I see what we really are.

I want to thank all the recruiters, HR pros, and hiring managers, and fellow geeks who generously gave me their time and thoughts. Without the input you all provided in our interviews on this topic, this book would not exist. I can't thank you enough for all your help.

For you recruiters, contact me through TimGoldstein.com and inquire how you can have Geeks Guide to Interview training to give to your candidates for free!

1 FUNDAMENTAL IDEAS AND CONCEPTS

Ideas and concepts

Before I jump into the top 3 interview winning strategies I thought it would be helpful to understand some of the ideas and concepts this book is founded upon. The first tenant is geeks, nerds and other technically orient people think differently than the general population. Not better or worse, just different. It is this different view which generates the ability for them to do the technical work, but makes it hard to share a viewpoint with them. Generally, this difference in thinking style is referred to as Neurodiversity.

To be a top candidate in a technical job search requires far more than raw tech savvy. It requires us geeks to step up and show we have functional "people" skills and use these abilities to showcase why we are the perfect fit. Fortunately, the level of skills needed to be successful in interviewing are limited in scope and can be revealed as straight forward methods that are easy to learn.

Here is a framework illustrating the different methods of thinking and how the neurotypical (NT)* non-tech interviewers consider far more than just the words in reaching an impression. It also illustrates the NT process frequently involves more factors including ones that are not easily quantified in an interview.

Geek Brain Processing

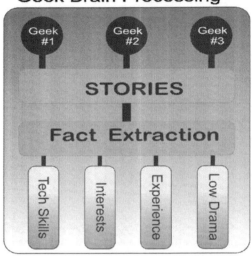

Neurotypical Brain Processing

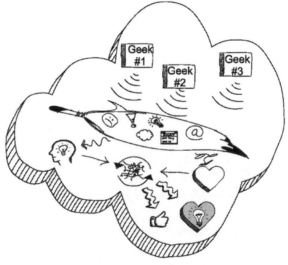

Another way to consider the difference in communication styles between Geeks and NT's is to consider what the Application Program Interface (API) calls to each for the same interaction looks like. Following are the different API structure to communicate your experience in a specific area to both audiences.

Geek:

Experience("Tech Fact")

Nuerotypical*:

Experience("Tech Fact", "Sound of Voice", "Appearance", "Soft Skills", "Physiology")

The proper API call to communicate with non-technical & neurotypical individuals requires more inputs which are not needed when making the same type call to a geek.

---

*Neurotypical or NT is the term used to refer to the majority of the populate who thinks in a typical manner. Usually they are social, chatty, and say what they feel will be accepted instead of what they really think. Neurotypical is just one possible arrangement of what I call the "Cloud" concept of Neurodiversity.

Get more Geeks Guide to Interviews resources at:
https://www.TimGoldstein.com/p/GGtI

2 TECH SKILLS, SMALL PART OF THE EQUATION!

Geek:

InterviewWin(Tech1, Tech2, Tech3, Tech4, Tech5)

Neurotypical:

InterviewWin(EnoughTech, Personality, Interests, Conversation, Feeling)

1.   The face to face interview is rarely about your tech skills

Normally before you get a face to face interview you will participate in a phone screen of your technical skill. This assessment of your technical abilities and knowledge are essentially the bar you need to get over to be considered for the position. Once you have cleared the bar, it is no longer your technical skills that will win the job for you. Yes, you may be asked more technical questions, but normally the purpose will be for different reasons than testing your tech skill.

The most common intent of additional tech questions after the initial tech screen tend to be as follows:

•　A potential coworker trying to figure out how you will affect their status in the group.

•　A manager or other non-technical oriented person. They normally want to hear you understand what they need and have the skills and experience to do the task. They don't want to be taught how to do it or the technical underpinnings.

•　A technically oriented hiring manager or higher level manager. They may ask or have the team ask you extremely difficult tech questions. Amazingly, this is not a test of your tech knowledge, but a test of how you problem solve and how you interact with and seek advise from teams or other resources

The best way to handle technical questions, after the tech interview, is to take a consulting approach by explaining your thoughts, as well as pros and cons of the various methods you think may answer the question. If you are unsure of the specific question always ask for clarification. This will not only make sure you answer the question correctly, it will also be taken as a display of emotional intelligence (EQ) which is highly valued by a non technical manager and HR.

Another important item is the length and depth you delve into as you answer. The best approach is to start at a high level and never talk for longer than 2 minutes although 1 minute is even better.

Now comes the most important step. Ask if you covered the question adequately or if they would like more detail. Frequently the overview is all they want, but if they do ask for more detail you are now in a position to ask them the specific area or details they want to hear more about. This has many benefits. One is simple math. If you ramble on about deep technical points for 5 minutes, during a standard 1 hour interview they can only cover about 10 questions. However, if you answer in small sound bites it matches how we now get most information. Most importantly it creates time for the interviewer to ask a much larger set of questions. It also keeps from branding you as someone who slows down meetings and decisions.

Never forget it is all about what you can do for them, not what is in it for you

•   According to the author of "The Perfect Interview" Dan Quillen, this is the most important thought to keep in mind. It also needs to be the foundation of all your answers. Your job at the interview is to clearly communicate how hiring you will benefit the company. This can be based on your experience, skills, personality, prior successes, etc. The important point is to always explain why what you have makes you the best person for the position.

•   There is an important question you need to ask to properly position yourself and identify your specific skills that will be a benefit to the company. Ideally, asking prior to the interview is best for preparation, but if not able to, ask as early in the interview as you are able. The question is "Why are you hiring for this position?". This question will let you know if their need is someone with great problem solving skills, the ability to be head down and crank out work, or to be a team builder who helps bridge the gaps with your skills. There are many other possibilities, but this gives you a good understanding of the type of information asking this question can get you.

Personality counts for everything

•   Once you have made it past the tech screen, the way you come across and how you make people feel are the keys to being the winning candidate. Being happy, upbeat, excited, and grateful are winning strategies. Coming off as negative, difficult, angry, or bitter will lose the interview the instant it appears.

Never talk negatively about jobs, people, managers, policy, pay or anything

•   There is nothing to be gained in an interview by talking negatively about anything. This is particularly true of experiences in your past whether it is a company, system, or person. The major red flag this type of speaking causes is a concern you will be negative and difficult to work with. A subtler, but possibly more powerful effect, is creating concern you will speak the same way about them and their company and systems.

Present a positive upbeat energetic persona

• People enjoy the energy and associate positive thoughts and attributes to people who are happy, positive, and energetic. While this may not be your nature, showcasing these traits during an interview is a skill you need to learn and use with everyone you interface with during the interview from the recruiter to the receptionist, and especially to the interviewers. It is not uncommon for the interviewers to ask the receptionist how you acted toward them. Anything but courteous, happy, and positive will cost you points when they start tallying up the pros and cons of each applicant.

Demonstrated problem solving is valued higher than any single tech skill

• Interviewers were virtually unanimous, having the ability to solve a problem is the number one skill they want. This one is virtually never in the job description, but it is in the mind of the people who have to work with and manage you. The thought is most IT challenges have many possible solutions and the job is to find the fastest one using the tools the company owns. While in some very specialized instances it is "Do you know how to do X with tool Y" it tends to be more in consulting and contracting when they are looking for a specialized skill set. For long term full time employment the ability to assess and solve a problem is far more important than knowing a specific command you could find on Google anyway. This is because the problems and tools keep changing so the ability to clearly show your problem solving abilities by talking through your thought process will always win you big points.

Get more Geeks Guide to Interviews resources at:
https://www.TimGoldstein.com/p/GGtI

3 STORIES PAINT PICTURES THAT WIN

Geek:

Story(Problem, Tech, Tech, GeekSpeak, AnotherTech, MoreTech)

NeuroTypical:

(Problem, Meeting, Solution, Decision, Challenges, Outcome, Leanings)

As tech people we tend to just "stick to the facts" when we explain something and say "just give me the facts" when asking questions. This works great when dealing with technical subjects, but not when trying to make a favorable impression on an interviewer. Most interviewers are of the neurotypical type who frequently gather their impressions and make decisions with a huge dose of how they feel putting emotional impressions over facts. This means if you want to make a lasting positive impression you have to make them feel something good about you. Stories are the key. A well-crafted story, even if only a minute long will make an emotional impression which will be long remembered and can deliver a few facts that will not be quickly forgotten. The goal when answering any non-technical question and even technical ones if possible, is to make the interviewer feel something.

Never answer with just Yes or No

In most tech environments the pace is fast and most true geeks, like myself and most others I work with, just want the facts as fast as they can get them. In these environments a "yes or no" answer works fine for many questions. But in an interview just answering "yes or no" is interpreted as a sign of low EQ. It also misses the mark in making the interviewer feel something from the answer other than short changed. Because of these reasons it is imperative the yes or no be delivered with more information than you are likely used to. As an example, if you are asked if you know XYZ program here are examples of a good yes and no response which will go much further to winning the interview.

Yes, I do know that program. I used it as a major piece in the solution the team I was on built for the accounting department. My role was as the primary developer working with that tool.

No, I have not had an opportunity in my prior experience to work with that tool. But I am very familiar and comfortable with program ABC which is the major competitor to XYZ. I am sure with the familiarity I have with ABC and already understanding the concepts these tools are based on, and I could very quickly transition to the package you use.

Create 60 - 90 second stories for each job on your resume

Every job on your resume needs to have a short story describing a brief high level overview of your position and duties, successes or innovations you were key to creating, and lessons you learned. This is not an autobiography, but a synopsis which is intended to convey the feeling you are competent, dedicated, and can be concise. This basic story should be memorized, but be delivered in a manner that sounds authentic. After delivering the story you need to ask if the answer was enough or if there are additional areas or details they would like to hear.

Story Structure

Good stories are structured to deliver maximum emotional impact and create the feeling you want others to get. While the words are important, it is even more important to structure the story for achieving maximum impact. The outline for the type of stories needed for interviewing are as follows in order:

Succinctly answer the question with a brief summation of the event or experience.

Describe the challenges you faced to accomplish or achieve what you described in #1.

Describe how you overcame the challenges to be successful.

If appropriate explain what you learned from the experience.

Here is an example of a story to answer the question, tell us about a time you had a conflict with a co-worker.

I was on a team assigned a project to create a new widget tracking system for the warehouse. While we were discussing approaches to the project I and a team member had a strong disagreement over the technology we would use to store the data. I was sure using NoSQL would create a better more flexible solution, but the other person was from a relational database background and not really up on NoSQL approaches and usage.

To help resolve the impasse I located some brief high quality comparisons of the 2 technologies and shared them with the entire team. I also created a super simple proof of concept using both technologies to demo to the team. At our next team meeting to discuss this issue I summarized the comparison and demonstrated both POCs. With the additional understanding we as a team were able to reach a consensus NoSQL looked like a more flexible solution and would be worth trying on this project.

What I learned from this is to make sure everyone has at least a high level understanding of alternate choices. I also learned a little time spent researching can save a lot of time arguing.

Does this cover what you are looking for or would you like more detail?

For reference, delivering this story at a comfortable pace for the listeners takes me about 60 − 70 seconds.

1 to 2 minute stories you must have

- Demonstration of problem solving

- About yourself

- Research first, but ask when needed to not spin wheels

- What you have accomplished

- What you are strong in

- Personal weakness

- Failed project, how you handled it and what you learned

- Conflict with a co-worker

Get more Geeks Guide to Interviews resources at:
https://www.TimGoldstein.com/p/GGtI

4 THE MAGIC WAND, SOFT SKILLS

Geek:

Communication(Mumble, LookAtFeet, Yes/No, Silence)

Neurotypical:

Communication(Smile, EyeContact, VoiceTone, FacialExpressions, Story)

Smile

• Nothing makes a neurotypical feel like you are friendly and likeable as a genuine warm smile particularly when you first meet. It doesn't matter if you like smiling or not. This is an absolute must when you first meet and at appropriate times through out the interview. So practice in front of a mirror until you can smile like you are truly enjoying the meeting experience.

Make them hear and understand you

• As star recruiter Natalie Zahn said, "I can't hire you if I can't hear you". An interview is not the place to be shy and meek when it comes to speaking. Talking softly causes a number of issues, both in physical hearing and worse in the perception you convey. If people ask you to repeat yourself or worse say they can't hear you well, you are talking far too softly. You need to speak loudly enough even the person furthest from you and sitting under the noisy vent can hear you clearly without straining. This level of volume serves to not only make you heard, but it also says you are confident. Talking softly makes the listener struggle to hear which is an unconscious mark against you. It also makes you appear as if you are not very confident or worse you are lying. While there are some people who talk too loudly, this is quite rare compared to being too soft. Although, it is something to watch for if your normal voice can be heard over jet planes taking off.

EQ Emotional Intelligents

•   This is one of the terms everyone says you need to have, but no one explains how they decide in an interview if you do. While interviewing the people who make this decision regularly I asked them how they judge whether you have it or not. Amazingly to me, it comes down to displaying a limited number of simple actions you can learn by rote. It does not require you to become an expert at reading body language and emotions which is a good thing for us geeks who just aren't wired to have these senses. Following is a list of some of the top actions which say you have ample levels of EQ.

1.   You must make at least parts of the interview a conversation where it flows back and forth between you and the interviewer like a tennis ball being volleyed.

2.   Ask a clarifying question occasionally such as "I just want to make sure I understand the question correctly, is it possible for you to ask that in a different way?"

3.   Keep your answers to an individual question in the 45 – 120 second range to avoid missing the signals you have gone on too long. Talking too much is a habit of most IT people except those who say only yes or no. Talking too long counts against you badly. Being short and then ask if you answered the question to their satisfaction wins every time.

4.   Eye contact is an absolute must. I understand many geeks have trouble with this. To the neurotypical types eye contact is a sign of honesty, openness, and showing respect.

If you struggle to make eye contact than try looking at the forehead just above the eyes. Interviewers will think you are making the eye contact they judge you by and you may be more comfortable than looking directly into their eyes. One thing to avoid with eye contact is maintaining it too long or intensely. Normally 3 – 5 seconds of eye contact then it is time to look at another interviewer or look down slightly as if you are looking inside for an answer. Do this and you will get major EQ points.

Get more Geeks Guide to Interviews resources at:
https://www.TimGoldstein.com/p/GGtI

5 WHO IS YOUR TEAM

API:

`NeedSupport({"TeamName"|"PersonName"}, "WhatNeeded", "NeedBy");`

While it may seem as if getting through an interview is a solo pursuit, it isn't. Unless you have been living under a rock and have no past you have a team either working for you or against you. All depends on recognizing it and using it. Your team is not just people, but also social media, resume, open sources contributions and more. All of these things can work for you or against you depending on how you use them.

On the people side, the biggest team member is the recruiter you are working with. If you are going it alone without a recruiter, you have given up a huge team asset. Recruiters are pros that work every day to get people matched up to jobs and through the hiring process. Unless you are the most ambitious unemployed person around, recruiters will have spent more time navigating the interview and hiring path in a week than you may have in your entire career. Yes, there are some terrible one's out there. I will cover finding the pros later. For now, just recognize a recruiter is your point person for your team and going without one is like a quarterback without a front line. Your resume will be sacked as often as that quarterback would be.

Other human team members are more like coaches, trainers, and all the support people that allow the quarterback to shine. Friends and co-Worker can be valuable in quite a number of ways. They can help you practice answering tech questions and if your network includes business side people you can even practice the soft side questions. Family can be a huge asset. Let's admit it, as geeks, little things like dressing with style can be a challenge. Family members who have that sense of style are a tremendous asset. I have always depended on my wife to help me coordinate my look so I convey a high-quality professional image instead of showing up as the unkempt geek in rumpled clothes.

Another group in the people category that is often unused is mentors. Yes, we are brilliant people or we wouldn't be able to do the technical work we do. But that doesn't mean we know everything in all subjects. A mentor can be invaluable if you want to cut your learning curve and get the real skinny on what works. If you are reading this, you are already using a mentor. I am telling you what works and what doesn't. Now you don't need to blow the interview for your dream job to learn how to be better at it. Where most of us geek types need mentoring is from someone in HR or a hiring manager on the business side. Consider contacting someone from a previous job in these type of positions and ask if you could buy them lunch and get interviewing advice. You will be amazed how helpful people can be when you ask them.

Anyone in your people team could be a link to the people who will be interviewing you. They might know them, be connected on social media, or know someone that knows them. We have all heard the old saying, it is not what you know but who you know. Might be sad, but it is oh so true. Never neglect asking your network including your social media network if they know anyone at the company you are interviewing with. Doesn't work every time but when it does it can grease your path. And remember your point person recruiter probably has these connections already!

Books and courses are virtual coaches. Someone took the time to put their wisdom or in my case the wisdom of many long term recruiters, hiring managers, and HR people into an easy to access form. Frequently hiring decisions come down to little differences. If you get one good tip from a book or course, that might be the difference between a new job and remaining where you are. The most important item to look at in books and courses is whether they come from people familiar with interviewing in the technical world or are oriented to the neurotypical types in non-technical areas.

The last group on your team is not humans. It is items like your resume, social media presence, LinkedIn profile, personal website or blog, GitHub or other open sources contributions, and any web presence that can be located with a search engine. This is becoming a more critical part of the team that will get you hired or not. If your social media presence is wild parties and activities which might not be illegal or immoral but don't sit well with the people interviewing you there is now a huge barrier to overcome. On the other hand, a solid LinkedIn profile with connections to people above your peer group will count on the plus side. Anything on the web that shows your involvement in positive non-controversial activities or groups will also be a big plus. Before you start your new job search I would highly recommend you clean up your online presence, get rid of the college party pictures and take down the postings in support of your favorite terrorist group.

I hope you now have the idea that like it or not you have a team. It is up to you to make sure your team has the right players and are all supporting you.

Get more Geeks Guide to Interviews resources at:
https://www.TimGoldstein.com/p/GGtI

Tim Goldstein

6 RECRUITERS ARE YOUR LIFELINE

API:

```
CareerChangeRequest("WhatIDo", "WhatIWantToDo", "EmploymentType",
"Skills", "SpecialTalents", "Rate", {"Availability"|"CurrentStatus"},
"ContactInfo");
```

Many of the geeks I know have a low opinion of recruiters and avoid communication with them. Comments I frequently hear are they pester you and waste your time. What this type of comment tells me is most geeks don't understand the role and value of quality professional recruiters, how to separate the good from the bad, and how to best utilize recruiters to reach your job goals. My own personal experience is I would not have the career or experience I do if it was not for my using and regularly networking with recruiters.

Let's start with the possible downside of working through a recruiter. When dealing with a good professional recruiter, there is really only one negative. It is a fact recruiters cost money, and some companies will not use them due to this added cost. While on the surface that seems like a downer, it can also be a positive because it weeds out companies that put money and cost in front of skills, experience, and ability. If the company is pinching pennies in the hiring process, you have to wonder where else they will try to trim costs.

The other downsides to recruiters are primarily with bad recruiters. Some will pressure you over positions that don't fit your career goals. Other will pester you incessantly with jobs that just don't fit your skills. My best advice is if you find these things happening you have been clearly told this is not a professional recruiter and is not on your team. Run from them as fast as you can.

Now I'll address how a quality professional recruiter helps you and is an invaluable member of your team. Pros know the market they serve and either know or can get details about a potential position up front that you would only figure out yourself once you interviewed assuming you can get an interview. This can be a tremendous time savings as you know up front what they are looking to pay and what they may stretch to if you are the perfect candidate.

You get background on the company and what the environment and culture is like along with many details you would never get such as what the manager is like. All of this through a comfortable conversation with someone that wants you to get a job that fits as much if not more than you do. A pro will work to understand where you are coming from and what specifically you want in a job for you to consider going to that company. Pretty much you get a career counselor for free which is a really good deal.

One of the biggest advantages of working with a recruiter is they have a relationship with the employers. The benefit of this to you is tremendous. To me, the number 1 advantage is a recruiter bypasses the HR software to get your resume seen by the hiring manager. If you want to go it alone, you will need to tweak your resume for every position to make sure you have the exact keywords and skills or the HR software will reject you before a human ever sees your resume. This can be a major bummer when you are a super good fit but didn't think like the HR person setting up the scanning software. Recruiters can get you interviews and even jobs you can't get on your own. I know of numerous examples where a direct call from the recruiter to the hiring manager either got an interview or a job offer. You can't do that on your own! If you get a job offer, the recruiter can be your agent in monetary and benefit negotiations. Pro sports players and entertainers use agents to negotiate these type of details for a reason. The recruiter likely has far more experience in these type of negotiations and a much better feel of how far to push without losing the opportunity.

The final item I want to discuss regarding recruiters is learning how to identify the pros that will help you from the amateurs that waste your time. These tips are what has worked for me. They are not perfect and just like any advice on picking a partner or mate will not guarantee you don't get a bad one. But they will put the odds in your favor and then just like dating you have to see where it goes.

My first stop is always LinkedIn where I look at how long they have been in the recruiting business. I am a pro and like you, top talent. I don't want my future in the hands of an amateur. If you are closer to entry level or lower mid-level, the people starting in a recruiting career can serve you well. But the higher up the career path you are, the more important it is to work with an equally seasoned pro.

The next item I consider which also comes from LinkedIn is where the person is located. Out of the country is into my deleted box. While I prefer local, I have had experienced pros in other states get me great gigs in my own town. So consider location in light of experience with experience being the most important aspect. I then look at how I was approached. If it is a form that I am supposed to fill out with my experience in some various categories, I am turned off. This is usually an indication of a body shop, meaning they don't care about you just about getting resumes to submit. Pros treat you as a professional, not a number.

If the recruiter has made it this far it is all about how they are and how I feel from a phone call. Once you find a few solid pros that want to work with you, stay in touch and let them know as your career desires change. A great recruiter is a long term relationship, and for me, a number have become valued advisers and friends.

Get more Geeks Guide to Interviews resources at:
https://www.TimGoldstein.com/p/GGtI

7 ASK QUESTIONS

API:

```
Question("AppropriateQuestion",                    "ProperTimeToAsk",
"ExpressionOfInterest", "ListenToEntireRespose");
```

There are numerous reasons and times for questions. Many of them are not to actually get an answer, but to convey a message in an indirect way. For those whatever the answer is, doesn't matter. What counts the most is conveying interest, excitement, or agreement with it. There are times when questions are expected. Not asking at these times is a mark against you in the soft skills area. Most interviewers will consider the lack of questions to be a lack of interest in the position. This makes it important to ask the right questions at the right time.

Always be prepared with genuine questions. Questions should center on why they are hiring for this position, team dynamics, what you will be doing, and company culture. While the answers to these questions might not really interest you, they are important to ask because of the message they convey. One of these messages is you are serious and prepared. Questions don't need to be complex. Simple questions like "What would my day be like?" or "How much of my day will be working with the team versus working on my own?" are great. You want to ask open-ended questions that cannot be answered yes or no. The goal is to get the interviewers talking, and questions that require description are exactly what you need.

There are some never ask questions. These questions may not get you disqualified, but it will raise red flags. Never ask about pay, benefits, time off, remote work, retirement, insurance or anything else that comes from the "What's in it for me" point of view. Never forget you are being evaluated for what you can bring to the company. During the interview is not the place to address these type of questions. First, they only matter if there is a job offer. Before then it is immaterial and because you have nothing to decide on the information is useless, and the message you gave the interviewers is you are not there for the company, but out for yourself. If a job offer is made you will have plenty of time to ask the "What do I get?" questions. It is appropriate and expected when an offer is made.

How do you handle the "Do you have any questions?" question if everything you had prepared was already covered? This is where having our questions written out in advance comes into play. Look up the list on your pad and go through it. Then look at the interviewer and say "I had a number of questions, but the interview process covered all the company and job items.". Now is the time to ask your closing questions. It is super important to ask a closing question as it tells them you are interested. I like these 2 closing questions. Your recruiter may have one they prefer you use, but here are some that work great.

Closing questions:

•   What are the next steps?

- Is there anything that would keep me from being effective in this position?

- Is there a further round of interviewing or will you be making a decision from this meeting?

By asking one of these closing questions you not only communicate you are interested in the position, you also get a 2nd chance to cover any concerns or gaps they may see.

Get more Geeks Guide to Interviews resources at:
https://www.TimGoldstein.com/p/GGtI

8 PHONE INTERVIEWS

API:

PhoneInterview("SolidConnection", "QuietLocation", "AdaquateTime", "ProperPreperation", "ConciseAnswers", ["ClosingQuestions"]);

Don't be fooled thinking a phone interview is any less important than a face to face version. If anything the phone interview is more important as it sets your first impression. When talking by phone, the interviewer has little to go on in deciding their impression of you.

One indicator used particularly by non-technical interviewers is your voice. This includes the actual sounds of your voice as well as your style of speaking. Talking too long convey you are hard to communicate with and don't listen. You will be branded with the label of long winded, and all the interviewers following will be looking for issues supporting this label even if it is not correct. You will make a first impression on your phone interview. It is up to you to learn the speaking skills to make it the impression you want.

For the actual interview call try to be on a dedicated phone line, not a cell phone. I understand this may be hard so if you must use a cell phone make sure you are in a quiet fixed location using a headset or earbuds. Don't do an interview call while you are driving. It is disrespectful to the interviewer(s) and distracting to you. You want to be at your peak for the phone interview and distracted driving combined with a distracted interview is a poor combination.

The phone interview frequently will be the main point of accessing your technical ability. It is frequently a technical person conducting the interview. My experience is the person doing the tech phone screen is not a frequent and studied interviewer. They may have a list of questions and they may not. Aim for a calm conversation as if discussing with your co-workers at Starbucks. Keep your answers short. It is best to give a short general answer then ask "Does that answer your question?". If yes, move on. If no they will usually indicate more specifically what they want which then makes it easy to answer.

Unless you absolutely know the interviewer wants the technical nitty gritty, the general then ask approach is the best way to handle any question where the depth of the desired answer is not clear. An additional advantage of this short answer approach is all the interviewer's questions can fit in.

Some other important thoughts around phone interviews are the same as face to face. Be prepared. Look at their website and understand how they make money. Do some Googling and find out what technologies they use and anything you can about the interviewer, the hiring manager, and the top IT executives. Prepare a list of questions that are ideally items about the work environment and culture.

Be sure to use probing questions as these replace visual body queues. If something is interesting to you, ask "Can you tell me more about that thing. It is an area of particular interest for me?". These types of open-ended probing questions will convey you have an interest as well as demonstrate soft skills that may not be natural for you. Asking about the interviewer's background and experience at this employer is another great soft skill builder but even more important it gives you a real in the trenches view of the company.

It is really important that you don't do all the talking. It counts negatively against you in the soft skills department and conveys you may not be a team player.

Get more Geeks Guide to Interviews resources at:
https://www.TimGoldstein.com/p/GGtI

9 INTERVIEW GOALS FOR INTERVIEWEE

API:

AccomplishGoal("Preparation","DeliverTheGoods","VerifyCorrectMessageReceived);

It is important to know what goals you must accomplish to win the current round of interviewing. Initially, the goal is to relay you are sufficiently skilled to match the position and that you seem likeable enough to work with. But as the interviews progress you may get feedback from your recruiter (this is a big loss when you aren't suing a recruiter) about a particular issue of concern or area it would be helpful for you to highlight. If you have the lecture of specific interview feedback, it is your first goal to address in subsequent interviews.

Lacking any specific issue to address the following are the standard items you want to strive to accomplish in every interview stage phone or face to face. First and foremost is to demonstrate technical ability in line with job requirements. Clearly, establish through questioning that you understand the job requirements. Questions like "What tools are used to create the reports that are part of this position?" will establish that you understand the job well enough to know it has a reporting requirement. You also want to hone in on your experience with the various tools in their stack of the competitive tools you have used. Once you have satisfied their belief you have the required skills, stop selling your tech skills and get on to the equally important goal of showing you are someone they would want to work with.

We are now in the frequently uncomfortable area of soft skills. There is a general though that tech workers don't have soft skills. There is also evidence this could frequently be true. What you need to do in the interview is not prove you are a soft skill genius, but that you have enough to be compatible with a team and easy to manager. Fortunately, much of this can be conveyed in a formula style approach that works whether you have the underlying soft skill or not. Here are the top soft skills goals:

- Create a human connection by asking questions that relate personally to the interviewer such as their own work area or the tools they use.

- Ask about the working environment and a normal day in the life of this position.

- Make it a consultive conversation by explaining multiple approaches or solutions that may work depending on the specifics of their architecture and environment.

- No BS, EVER. They must feel they can trust you with everything you say. If you only have light experience in something be sure to say something like "I only have a limited amount of experience with that tool but enjoyed it."

For me, this is one of the most interesting areas of the interview process. It is the items the employer wants to know but can't ask due to legal restrictions and company policy. But just because they can't ask doesn't mean they won't be making guesses then decisions on those guesses. Following are some of the most common questions they would like answered:

- Do you have a level of commitment to stay at least 18

months to 2 years?

- What is your social life like and will it bring negative influence or habits to the workplace?

- How you are outside of the office when you interact with friends, family, store clerks, bad drivers, etc?

- Can you deliver the work needed at an acceptable quality level and keep the users and stakeholders informed of progress and delays?

- Are you able to work comfortably and enjoyably across age, business line, gender, or any other type of divisions?

The best way to answer these unaskable questions is to weave their answers into the answers for the questions you are asked. For instance, when they ask about why you are leaving your prior job you can add in you are looking for a place to call home for the next couple of years at least. When asked about your strengths talk about how you are really good at delivering quality work on time and keeping the customer informed if for some reason you will be late. The more answers to the unaskable questions you can mix in the stronger your human connection will be.

Get more Geeks Guide to Interviews resources at:
https://www.TimGoldstein.com/p/GGtI

10 COMMUNICATING YOUR BRAND

API:

MyBrand("HowYouLook,""HowYouSound,""HowYouAct," "KeyTraitsOrSkills")

Brand is something we rarely think of in regards to ourselves. It is a great concept to consider and understand. Presenting ourselves as a brand creates interest and delivers a consistent, intentional message. Think about political candidates. They normally have 3 or 4 items they always come back to. This anchors themselves as being or representing these items. It is a great way to have yourself thought of.

If your brand is creative problem solving, professional demeanor, and you get the job done and deliver you need to be making and reinforcing these points at every appropriate opportunity in the interview. Just think what the results would be if everyone you interviewed agreed on who you are. This is the power of brand.

Brand is an entire study by itself. I will only be covering a few of the points. Begin by deciding what brand you is all about. I think of brand as an equation. One side is who we say we are and on the other how do we act. Stronger brands are those where the equation equals and they do what they represent. I purposely chose the image at the start of this section. It may help me explain the next part. I hope everyone agrees that image would not be appropriate anywhere around professional. Why? I think because it does not speak a message of professional. Okay, pro partier, but not pro technical talent. The point is for you to present a strong brand you must choose your brand then make sure everything sees, hears, feels, smells consistent. Getting to the point, becoming your brand involves basing everything you do and say on what you have decided you are.

The view from my Asperger's perspective is these are the most important areas to be consistent and form a strong brand:

- Appearance Static, what you look like just standing or sitting there.

- Appearance Dynamic, how do you move, quickly with intent and confidence or meekly as if you are about to be beaten.

- Vocal Qualities, how your voice sounds. What tone, what pitch, what pace?

- Speaking Ability, how you use the sounds you make to express yourself.

To become your brand may require help. Find someone that knows style and ask them to help you get together an interview outfit and all the pieces to complete it. Belt, shoes, jewelry, the works. That fixes you up for looking consistent. Moving can be difficult to learn, but can be learned. Basics of stand straight, no hunching, looking at eye level, not the floor go a long way. To really ace this one requires coaching for some odd sources. Yoga, dance, acting are all great ways to learn more about how your body moves and how to move your body to communicate your message. Vocal and speaking ability when taught by the best is learning the first steps to being a singer. My coach has a great training series for speaking, and he coaches the best. Go to http://www.RogerLove.com or check out his YouTube channel to get a bunch of free lessons.

Now that you know why being your own brand is so important and have some ideas to implement the question is, will you do it? While it is considered normal to just be yourself in the IT department or design department, it is not the norm in most business. Are you willing to let go of some of your freedom to be whomever you want at work to be highly employable and able to direct your own career?

Get more Geeks Guide to Interviews resources at:
https://www.TimGoldstein.com/p/GGtI

11 PREPARE OR DIE

API:

Success("Preparation", "Timing", "Presentation", "Qualifications");

Life or interviews, the best way to get a jumpstart is preparation. In today's employment environment it is common for the decision to come down to fit. Do you fit the company, department, and team culture? The best way to do well on fit is preparation and studying the company. This allows you to ask specific questions which also demonstrate your interest in the company. It also shows soft skills due to the interest in the culture.

Preparation comes from a variety of sources. The intent is not to make preparation a project requiring every bit of information from every source, but to learn what you can, using an appropriate amount of time to the importance. If you missed one page on their website, there is no penalty. Your goal is to integrate and assimilate bits from all the sources into as comprehensive a view of the company as possible. I know this sounds time consuming, but we are going to time box it and give it a couple of hours' tops.

There are 2 areas of preparation, "You" and research. The "You" portion deals with creating story style answers for the common questions you know they will ask. Next, create questions that relate to a top or item that takes a little effort to find. Maybe something from a press release or outreach program that ties to one of your interests. Something like, "Can you tell me about the company supporting the Cure Everything Foundation as they are a big cause of mine?"

Following, are the main "You" items to work on:

- Write down the story style answers for the hard questions you hope they don't ask.

- Practice Interviews.

- Create a list of questions you want to ask.

The research part is mostly a couple hours on the web searching and reading about the company and maybe the industry it might also be a few phone calls. It is not a quick look between game sessions, but serious research to equip yourself to get a job offer. Following are primary items to research.

- Research the company. What do they do? How big are they? Where are their locations? How are they regarded in the industry?

- Know high level, how they make their money and the business model.

- Research the opportunity. What specifically is the position? What are the responsibilities? Is travel required? How big is the team or group you would work on? Above all, know the job description.

- Find out the compensation for both your local market doing the same duties as similar companies and for the specific opportunity.

- Read ALL the company website particularly looking for items related to culture and causes.

- Look at the company and interviewers on LinkedIn.

- Check out the company on Glassdoor.

- Contact your network and see if there is anyone that works there you can talk with or knows about the company.

When it comes to how to prepare, you can't beat the old fashion writing it down. If you have been struggling with your list of questions to ask at the interview, this can be your treasure trove. Even if you already believe you understand the answer just saying "From the website, I believe the company does XYZ. Am I correct about this?" will go a huge way in establishing a higher level of emotional intelligence than may be common. Besides the most obvious source of Google, here are a number of resources that are useful to research a company:

- Recruiter
- Company Website
- LinkedIn
- Glassdoor
- Annual Reports
- News articles
- Your network

If you are looking for long term ways to improve yourself and your preparation, consider studying or even buying some online course on improving your story writing and telling skills. When you are able to give a clear message in a compelling manner, your relatability and soft skills impression increases immensely. Find opportunities to interact with new people and groups even when it is uncomfortable. New ideas frequently come with new people. This will also force you to practice your soft skills.

Get more Geeks Guide to Interviews resources at:
https://www.TimGoldstein.com/p/GGtI

12 THE MAGIC WAND, SOFT SKILLS DEEP DIVE

API:

```
SoftSkillEvaluator("OverallFeel,"    "Present,"    "Aware,"    "Personable,"
"LowFriction");
```

Soft skills are a magic wand and your best way to stand out among your technical peers. As someone with Asperger's, I also understand how hard it can be to try and navigate all the little rules of soft skill magic. In interviewing the people who decided if you get the job, I found some simple steps, rules, and processes which are easy for our logical minds to follow, but which say "Emotional Intelligence" to the interviewers.

The most important item for you to accomplish may be the hardest. You must learn interview etiquette and then follow it like a script. I'm an Aspie, so I understand how hard some of these can be. But this is a situation where you need to stretch and do some things you may not like.

The first 30 seconds are the time to create the impression of the type of person you are. First, let's consider what traits and action are well received.

- Friendly

- Happy

- Confident

So how do you give this impression in 30 seconds? You need to do it with your voice and body language. People like others who are happy and grateful which makes them seem friendly. So the question is how do you sound and look happy and grateful? It is easier than you think and you only need to pull it off for 30 seconds or so. Happy people speak and move faster. Their pitch goes higher, and their face shows smiling signals from the cheeks and eyes. Switching to grateful is very easy. Just slow your pace and hold the words while using a little lower, stronger tone. If this is just not making sense, you may want to see it on one of our videos.

How else can you convey your grasp of soft skills?

- Smile. This could be the most important thing you do. Before meeting anyone, think of something that made you happy, excited, and smiling. Now think of that and let your body just be excited and smiling just like you remember. While there is nothing wrong with continuing in this light friendly demeanor, if it is a struggle, just 20 or 30 seconds of it will make a great impression.

- Give them a feeling. I know, I am an aspie too. How do you give something you don't even get insider your own body? This is a very important aspect of being the right candidate. Here are a few items that will help greatly in giving the proper positive feeling.

    o Learn to give an excellent handshake. Firm and about 3 seconds.

    o Look directly at the eyes of the person you are speaking to. If this is too hard, just look between their eyes as a single point. They will not know you aren't looking in their eyes.

- o Confident never cocky.
- o Make it clear you are excited about the job and opportunity.

Traits, habits, and items you want to avoid at all costs.

- Arrogance is a loser, and no one wants to work with an arrogant person.

- Appearing overly introverted creates team fit concerns. Ask questions, interact.

Following is a list of additional items that interviewers will be considering at to judge your soft skills.

- Self-motivated and easy to manage.

- Open to learning and advice.

- Knowledgeable about a range of topics, not just tech.

- Speak loudly enough to be heard and clearly enough to be understood.

- Analogies to explain concepts making it easier for others to relate.

- How you look and move counts. Don't walk like a sloth.

- Have a professional interview outfit that includes well-maintained shoes.

- Interaction must happen. If you don't create a back and forth discussion by asking clarifying questions, it will be hard to be considered personable.

- Ask if your answer adequately addressed the question.

- Awareness of others non-verbal cues.

- Willing, able, capable. The message you must project.

Get more Geeks Guide to Interviews resources at:
https://www.TimGoldstein.com/p/GGtI

13 TOP FACE TO FACE INTERVIEW MUST DO'S

API:

F2FInterviewEvaluator("HowDidIFeel","AppropriateAnswers","Communicatio nkSkills", "Authentic", "EasilyManaged", "ProblemSolvingSkill");

The big deal you have been working toward is finally here. You have cleared the many different preliminary steps from updated resume to tech screen. You like what you have heard, and they want to meet you face to face. Congratulations!

What will the interviewers be looking for? What should I be concerned about? OMG, I have to be with people in the same room looking at me? You have it exactly, the dog and pony show formal interview. This is the place where you can stand out from the other candidates based on your ability to deliver a well-crafted message conveying why you are the best choice. It is critically important to remember that everything about you gives a message and they all need to say the same thing!

Like it or not people make decisions about you from what they see in the first few moments. Think about this as an evolutionary ability to size up friend or foe. To be instantly judged "friend" you need to fit in comfortably and authentically. Here are some suggestions for your initial impression.

- Dress appropriately for company and position

- Dress includes haircut, facial hair, and social/cultural grooming standards

- Dress one step up from the job you want to have, not your current job

- Do not overdress and appear you will not fit in

- Geeks are given slack in dress, but still important to not be over or under dressed

If you don't have an idea what attire would be appropriate a great resource it to ask the recruiter or HR contact for their attire advice. If you are totally desperate go with this generic dress suggestion:

- Men, button down shirt, slacks, and dress shoes. Tie and sport coat optional depending on company culture.

- Women, Professional dress skirt not too short and a nice blouse.

- My own personal advice for us guys, wear pink shirts.

Now that you have gotten over the idea of some new clothes and a general clean up, I am going to move on to a number of items which some of us techie/geekie/Aspie types may find uncomfortable. Sorry to say, but this is where you have to suck it up and make yourself do it the way the employers want. Deliver on these, and you will have a good interview.

- Be on time

  This means at the front desk 5 – 10 minutes in advance. Don't be more than 10 minutes early. Walk around the block if you have to. NEVER be late.

- Smile

  If you read Dr Rich Castellano's book "The Smile Prescription" he will give you the medical studies and his own experience as a plastic surgeon about why you should be smiling anyways. But if you want to win the face to face interview you need to smile more and be happier than the people interviewing you. People are drawn to happy people and smiling is a way of saying you are happy.

- Make eye contact

  I'm an Aspie, I get it. This can be physically painful and disrupt my ability to talk. I am not the one that made it this way, but most humans expect direct eye engagement. It is taken as a sign of authenticity and honest. Don't give this to your interviewers and you will always be suspect as foe. You can fake it and don't even have to look into their eyes. Just look at a spot between their eyes and continue looking as you speak for 3 – 5 seconds. Then look away or at others in the interview and return back to the person asking the questions. Everyone gets eye contact and is happy. Guess what you are still alive. Might have been hard and scary, but you can do it.

- Look open, approachable, friendly

  One part of how you appear was discussed above as clothing and grooming. This addresses the other part of how you appear, your physical posture, presence, gestures, and the way you move. Here are some simple steps you can take to emanate a good vibe. Stand or sit tall, no slouching. Don't bring so many things it is difficult to shake hands with you. Did I mention smiling? No arms or hands crossed in front of your body.

- Warm sincere happy friendly greeting

  Look directly at people and say "Hello" in a strong enough voice to be easily heard and understand. Use happy, excited tones in your voice. Use melody, no one likes monotone, ever.

- Be up front if you are nervous

  Guess what, the other people in the room are human also. They get nervous when they are the one being interviewed. It is fine to say up front that you are a little nervous, then don't bring it up again. They will remember, and you don't need to keep telling them and yourself how nervous you are. Or, just press on knowing they already expect you to be nervous and you don't want to disappoint.

- Displays willingness to adapt to company culture

  I know, we techies, geeks, and Aspies know the right way to do something and are glad to show you. But if you want a job offer it is far more important to show your ability to relate and adapt to their company culture. You can leverage the interviewers' explanation of how they do things by responding with comments like "That is something I wished other companies considered in their culture." or "I have always wanted to work for a company which agreed that aspect is important." Take any chance you have to show agreement or desire for their unique cultural elements.

- Demonstrate your skills fit the needs they have

  I hope you haven't forgotten, the interview is all about what is in it for the company. The most important thing in it with the proper hire is a person with the skills they need. Not just the skills on the job description, but all the ones they don't list but many lack. If you are really good at cross-department communication, tell them about a time that skill won the day. If they are hiring for a tech lead and it is obvious they need some project management help, tell about the project you informally took over managing. Always explain how your specific experience with the skill makes you the perfect fit for their similar need.

- Ask questions

  As one recruiter told me, the most important thing about

questions is to have some. This is your chance to add or clarify anything you feel would improve your chances. Ask for more about a project or initiative they mentioned which interests you. Ask "Is there anything that makes you feel I would not be successful in the position?" Whatever you ask, make it something which requires them to tell you more. There are a few areas to not ask about at an interview. Bluntly, don't ask "What's in it for me?" questions. No asking about salary, benefits, or perks. Instead ask questions about them, their needs, their goals.

Get more Geeks Guide to Interviews resources at:
https://www.TimGoldstein.com/p/GGtI

14 INTERVIEW NEVER DO'S

API:

AbortInterview("OverallFeel,"   "Present,"   "Aware,"   "Personable,"
"LowFriction");

Don't judge this list by exception. It is possible to do some of these and sometimes still get hired. None of the items mentioned will add any value to you as a candidate. But any one of them can get you taken off the list. So why risk losing out on a great job?

- Never be late

Arrive on time means 5 – 10 minutes before your appointment time. Arriving late says lots of things about you, and none of them are good.

- Never talk negatively about Companies, managers, co-workers

Even if you work for Attila the Hun, your co-workers backstab for weekly points, and the company has a hard time finding something they do legally, you only talk about them in the context of positive benefits or learnings. You can easily do this by describing the scenario high level in general terms. No editorial. Now and most important, tell what you learned from it and how useful that concept is for you.

- Never appear arrogant or condescending

This one can be hard for some of the Aspie crowd due to the inability to discern these traits. While it can occasionally come from the words you use, that is pretty obvious, and you can make other word choices. Mostly, this is a tone of voice and body language thing. The best way to get a handle on this is video tape yourself doing a mock interview. Then study it. Get someone you trust to give honest answers, not a geek, to critique you for these traits. While you may be terrible at the whole body language, tone of voice thing, the easy thing here is you just need to learn to avoid a few specific combinations. No acting involved.

- Never answer as a scripted monotone

Really 2 issues rolled up into one here, and both are very prevalent in the techie crowd. One issue is scripted, and the other is monotone or worse, monoresonant.

Scripted happens when you try to remember exact words and sentences to say. Except for some super actors, it will come across as if you are reading words you are not emotionally attached to. The best way around this is to create your stories around bullet points and questions. Then when you tell that story, you are going through it again, and it comes out as real.

I think we all know what monotone is. That droning on that just keeps going on the same note over and over. Monoresonant is monotone combined with no change in the other 4 components of your voice, pitch, pace, volume, tone, and melody either. It is as dull and lifeless as you can get. If you can imagine a bored zombie talking, it would have about the same sense of excitement. If when you listen to your voice mail message and don't even like it yourself, it is time to consider some vocal help. Try checking out http://RogerLove.com who is my vocal coach and creator of huge amounts of both free and paid training. He can help change you from high pitch, grate on your nerves geek voice to a strong, solid voice that conveys the message you want just like he did for me.

• Never denigrate the technology stack or current systems

Always think of your face to face interview as if you were visiting someone's home. If your style is southwestern and you walk into a home that is done as New England cottage, you wouldn't start telling them why your style would suit them so much better. But this is exactly what you do when you say anything against the technology and tools (decor) of the company you want to hire you. Just like picking on a host's tastes will probably not get you invited back, picking on the company's technology tastes is the same.

• Never assume who in the room is important. Be respectful to everyone especially support staff

It is not at all uncommon for some of the more involved decision makers to take a passive role in an interview. They may be assessing team and personnel skills while they are forming an opinion on you the candidate. Because of this they will let the team ask the questions and run the interview. Never assume just because someone hasn't spoken they are not important. Treat everyone in the room as important and give each one eye contact and direct attention as you speak. Direct the majority of your answer to the questioner, but make sure everyone gets attention.

Never forget that any staff you deal with could be providing input about you. It is not unusual for the receptionist to be asked how you acted. In one high-tech company, they even have the driver that takes you to and from the airport give input on how you behaved. No need to be paranoid, but be aware and treat everyone like you should anyways.

Get more Geeks Guide to Interviews resources at:
https://www.TimGoldstein.com/p/GGtI

15 PROPER ETIQUETTE WHILE ON THE COMPANIES' PREMISES

API:

PositiveEtiqutte("Appearance", "Manners," "Role," "Decorum");

You want to think about being at the interviewers' physical location almost like a visit to a foreign culture. Meaning, they will have different expectations and different interpretations of your actions. You have no control how they will interpret anything. Most things you can easily handle on the fly. Just make any question into a dialog. Ask questions, be engaged. Here is advice for a few frequently asked areas:

- Cell Phone

    The overwhelming advice is your cell phone is best left it in the car. There are many reasons for this from the practical to the psychological. Having your phone sends a signal saying the interviewers are not as important as something else. Practically it is one more thing in your hand that can become a barrier between you and greeting another person.

There are very few exceptions to the no cell phone rule. The 2 situation which comes to mind are a serious personal situation you are waiting for a difficult to return call or you are on call for your current position and could be called during the interview. If you have a situation like this, the best thing to do is apologize at the opening of the interview and give a brief description of the situation, no details.

- Beverage or Refreshment

This one can be confusing as it can vary by the culture of the organizations. Unless there is something strongly indicating otherwise, I would stick with these conservative and safe guidelines.

  o Do not carry one in with you

    This speaks pretty clearly, you are taking the interview casually. If it is summer in Denver, you might not raise an eyebrow if you carry in a bottle of water. But a Starbucks any place except maybe interviewing at Starbucks is just a bad idea. This is another item which can get in your way when you need to greet and shake hands.

  o If offered always accept graciously

    If you are offered a beverage, always say yes and take water. Water is safe because if you spill it is not the disaster of other liquids and it makes the decision a fast, easy process.

  o If not offered, it is acceptable to ask for water

    It is very convenient to have a bottle or glass of water during the interview. It is a great prop when you need a little time to consider your answer to a question. With the modern understanding of hydration, it is not considered abnormal or negative to ask for water. Best time to ask is after the introductions, but before everyone is settled. Just politely ask "Would it be possible to have some water?"

• Bio Breaks

This can definitely be a difficult and embarrassing issue to deal with. First, you need to fully recognize every human has the same needs, so it is not strange. Next, realize how poor your concentration can be when your body is screaming at you about important tasks you need attending to.

○ Best approach is take care of it before the interview

You know when you are trying to figure out what to do with yourself from when you arrive until it is time to walk to the receptionist. Find a bathroom and take care of that extra coffee. It is also a great chance to look in a mirror for a last once over, just to make sure you don't have something that makes you look embarrassing. A trick that might help, on many multi-tenant office, building the restrooms on the main floor will be locked. If you can get up a floor or two, they are normally open.

○ If a long interview without a break it is okay to politely ask

This especially happens when it is one of the meet this person, then to this person, then to... type interviews. Each one of them may have you for a whole hour. But for you this could be your 3rd hour in a row and the yellow tint is making it hard to clearly pick up the interviewer's body language. Try to pick a natural break such as changing interviewers. But if it is pressing, be human and admit you could think more clearly if you could take care of this little distraction.

Get more Geeks Guide to Interviews resources at:
https://www.TimGoldstein.com/p/GGtI

16 BEST WAYS TO RUIN AN INTERVIEW

There are many ways to accomplish things and some ways that are particularly effective. While there are likely other great ways to ruin an interview, these are some of the most common interview killers the people making the decisions run into.

- Swearing

    This one is guaranteed to only have a downside. Swearing will not improve your standing or potential of getting an offer, but it sure will bring up questions about your demeanor and attitude.

    Best thing to do is not swear. I understand that particularly in the younger generations many words that were considered swearing have entered the common vocabulary. This is one place you are safest going with tradition. If it was considered an offensive word in the last few decades, handle it that way now. Don't use it.

- Being defensive

This can be a difficult one to overcome particularly for the technical Aspie type. It occurs most frequently when you are questioned about a decision. As an Aspie, I generally interpret that as a questioning of my skills and react poorly. What I have learned is, I need to look at this as a thought exercise.

Pretty much, based on what you now know, would you have followed the same thought process and decisions? Then talk through it from the consulting learning perspective. Do be aware and consider if the environment is one where being on the defensive is part of the culture. If so does that work for you?

- Disparaging the company's technology stack and processes

Yes, you have great experience, and you have worked on projects and systems that were successful for high profile customers. You have a bag of tricks which work really well for you. In the interview, you find out they use a technology stack that does not fit your bag of tricks. The absolute worst thing you can do is try to impress the company with your brilliant tricks and how it will fix all the problems with the technology they use.

Remember they have a huge amount invested in that technology, and some of your interviewers have part of their career built on it. Saying their technology choices were bad and they need your or some other super new approach is about like telling a new mother her baby is ugly. Hopefully, you'll live through it!

- Being late

We have talked about the importance of being on time and what we mean by that. If you blow it on this one, it is often an automatic no. Even if they allow the interview, you will be at a huge deficit due to your need to convince them you are a responsible adult that takes time and commitments seriously.

- Taking a phone call

We covered the only 2 reasons to take a call. We covered that the phone is best in the car if you aren't in an emergency call situation. Answering a call which you haven't warned your interviewers about is the same as standing on the conference table and announcing "no matter what my life is first."

• Being egotistical

Bluntly, no one wants to work with a jerk. While most tech fields are very accepting of the personality quirks, egotism, conceit, self-centeredness, devaluation of others are all red flags for long term problems. As geeks, techies, and Aspies we can easily be perceived this way due to our tendency to know everything and then want to tell everything about it.

The other way we project this is with our voice and the spirit we answer and discuss in. This will likely take asking someone you trust that has good people skills to critique and suggest changes. You need to find out if you sound or act egotistically. If so do whatever it takes to.

• Implying the job is not the preferred choice

Your good, your connected, and you have other job opportunities in the pipeline. The interview goes well, and at the end, they ask you if this is a position that would interest you. The answer is always "Yes" unless you never would work there if it was the last place on earth. The worst answer is "No the position with Acme is my first choice. But if it doesn't happen I would consider this one." You have just done everything possible to tell them you have no engagement with their culture or mission and all you want is the most you can for yourself.

• Extensive "What's in it for me?" questions.

I understand you want to get the details like what is the salary, benefits, can you work from home, the holidays, do you pay for education, etc. These are all important, and you will need to know them before you consider accepting the position.

But they haven't offered you anything yet! You are still in the "What's in it for them" stage where you are showing them all the reasons you are the perfect solution. If this interview progresses to a job offer, you will then be at the right stage in the process to ask all these questions. If you have taken my preferred approach of working with a quality recruiter, you can frequently get a lot of these details without sounding as if you only care about what you get.

Get more Geeks Guide to Interviews resources at:
https://www.TimGoldstein.com/p/GGtI

I ADDENDUM – HOW ASPERGER'S / HFA SHOWS UP AT WORK

If you haven't knowingly been around a person with Asperger's it is quite likely you will not recognize it. Instead you will consider the person to be quirky at best and as a leading CEO's of the time put it, "a brilliant jerk" at the worse. Following are numerous short vignettes. While no one is indicative of anything, if you find a few of these ringing true and normal is seeming a little strange, you may want to consider approaching the person using some of the techniques that seem to work well with those on the spectrum.

I have also included a few vignettes from the perspective of the person with Asperger's. Mostly these views draw on my own experience and how I processed the situation. The purpose is many of us over 30 who are on the spectrum have never been diagnosed. We usually know life is a little different for ourselves, but never catch on why. My diagnosis with Asperger's tied a thread through so many aspects of my life which I never saw connected. My wish is that if you are undiagnosed and some of these ring a bell, you will dig in further. Maybe you will find the thread that pulls your life together like I did.

1. You need a little change to your project. You approach Ted the tech person on your project, and greet him. The response is a cold flat, "Yes?" Ted, we need to have you make a little change in the project. Ted becomes defensive and agitated. The changes are explained and at every step Ted is pointing out the challenges, extra work, and how badly it will mess up the program architecture. Your meeting done, Ted reluctantly agrees to work on the changes. Ted goes off complaining about them screwing up my design and you're worn out from so much energy spent in a simple change.

2. Your system has a quirky issue which is driving you nuts. You put in a help desk ticket on the intranet. The tech arrives looking as if this could be the 2nd week for his outfit. With a distant arrogant tone he asks "What's the issue?" Other than the words, everything else about him said "What did you do to break it?"

3. You just learned a new approach which would be a great added enhancement to an almost completed project. You explain the small changes and they react with overwhelm. Every item is turned into a complex web of steps required. As you point out the positives of making the change they become obviously anxious and overwhelmed as they try to understand all the ramifications.

4. The engineer is asking for everyone's input on the new project. You describe a need you perceive. The engineer then asks about more details. You describe what you know. You then continue to be interrogated, "Do you mean this?", "Is it only this and can never be that?", "Could this condition ever occur?" The questions all sound as if they are asking the same thing and you have already answered. When is this jerk going to get it that you just plain don't know what he is asking and what answer he is expecting?

5. Your boss is brilliant, but frequently quite a jerk. They came up through the technical ranks where they excelled. But dealing with them in a leadership role is draining. Unrealistic demands. Responses which insult your skills, and drain your enthusiasm. Need a technical solution and your boss has the perfect approach. Try to get anything done about the person in the department that is not pulling their weight. Nothing happens and you feel further isolated and singled out to live in an unreal world where nothing seems to work normally.

6. You mention to one of your technical co-workers about a gaming gadget your daughter is asking for. While you were hoping for some advice and a suggestion, you instead got an education about everything involved down to melting the sand to make the chips. You tried every nice, not so subtle, and plain out right obvious attempts to get out of the conversation to no avail. You are now trapped in the Asperger's special interest zone.

7. There is a guy in engineering you need to meet with regularly for your project. Nice enough guy. Low key, easy going if somewhat introverted. Not super talkative, but communication is plenty clear for the project needs. One big issue. When you must meet in the little huddle rooms the smell from his rumpled and unkempt clothes combined with body odor make the meeting almost impossible to attend.

8. You manage technical employees and in preparing reviews you found quite a dilemma with one of your most outstanding technical team members. On one hand they have been productive, contributing to everyone on the team, proposes innovative and functional solutions. But the issues are piling up, customer complaints about his aloofness, attitude and careless statements, and when given multiple tasks there just seems to be no ability to prioritize and get work done.

9. Your conversing with a techie. Nothing life and death, but a topic with multiple perspectives. You try to discuss your disagreement on points, but never get to have the conversation. You are arrogantly talked over as the techie goes off deeper and deeper into why their view is right and all the support for it. You give up conversing and just hope to escape with your ears attached.

You may tend to the Asperger's arrangement of neurodiversity if some of these scenarios resonate with you.

1. You're a tech worker on a project rolling out a new release. Things go wrong and as the only one still there you are pulled into firefighting this issue and getting service restored. It's a nightmare. You know your part well, but there are so many other pieces and technologies. No one from the other teams are available. Suddenly it seems the world is depending on you. Your anxiety kicks in. You feel stressed and pulled past your limits. You want to deliver and look good for the whole team. There is so much you don't know. You have a project manager in your cube pushing for an answer to when it will be fixed. Your stress and anxiety are off the chart and the shut down on the way to a meltdown is kicking in. You cut off as many of the distractions as you can and focus everything on the issue. The PM is back and pushes harder for a resolution date. This one extra demand of giving a firm answer for an unknown problem finally does it. You meltdown, cursing, over generalizing, angry, frustrated. Like lava flowing out of a volcano, hurt, anger, retaliation, and rationalization comes out of you.

2. You're the specialist for a technology in this project. You're told to find the best version and standards. You research and come up with some great solutions. Every one you present is turned down by some department for some incomprehensible reason. Time running out and a decision is made to just use the old technology you were brought in to replace. The manager tells you the plan. Just use the old stuff and build on top of it. Your head starts reeling as you start thinking through all the changes required, the architecture, the code, the skills needed,

the time, your anxiety. Every road is a dead end and soon shutdown follows. Your brain just cannot process any more moving, unpredictable, unstable situations.

3. You're being interviewed for a technical position and the interviewer is a manager from a business group you would be supporting. You have honed your tech skills and want to let this manager know the depths of your technical knowledge. Every time they ask a question you are sure to give you understanding of the subject in the technical terms that cover it. The manager continues to question fluff knowledge and what you do on the playground and doesn't even acknowledge your technical mastery.

II ADDENDUM – WHAT IS ASPERGER'S, HFA?

Image via creative commons license from the Flickr photostream of DailyPic

History

This is a very condensed high level view of the history from my perspective as a person with Asperger's but no medical authority on the subject. For an in depth study, see Steve Silberman's well research book "Neurotribes".

Asperger's Syndrome is named for Hans Asperger. He was an Austrian physician, medical professor, and pediatrician. He identified a group of children he referred to as his "Little Professors". It was from this small group that Dr Asperger first described the condition now known as Asperger's Syndrome.

During the period from WWII and continuing for decades, Asperger's was not even recognized as a condition. In the USA there was an ongoing battle over who discovered autism and the specific criteria to determine what was seen as a childhood condition. This battle and Asperger's work not being translated to English until the 90's cause the condition to remain unknown. It wasn't until the early 90's that Asperger's Syndrome was recognized as a disorder of children.

Most studies and diagnostic criteria are based on children and the behaviors they exhibit. This is understandable with the recognition Asperger's is not outgrown, but takes on different traits and manifestations as a person matures. Because of the inclusion of these childhood traits many adults with Asperger's do not meet a clinical criteria for diagnosis, but functional they are well into the neurodiverse cloud that ends as Asperger's, or as we say, on the spectrum.

Asperger's Syndrome was combined into Autism Spectrum Disorder (ASD) in the DSM 5 and is now referred to as High Functioning Autism (HFA). I stick with the older Asperger's name as to me it is more descriptive of the general traits I discuss and less vague than HFA.

Autism in general is believed to be a pervasive developmental syndrome caused by the physical structure and wiring of the brain. The alternate structure and wiring appear to cause the brain to process and function differently as well as creating a disconnect from emotional processing. Pervasive refers to the symptoms expressing in many ways and parts of daily life.

Because of the narrow diagnostic standards including items such as "Repetitive hand movements (e.g., clapping, finger flicking, flapping, twisting)", which as an adult I have learned not to do, Asperger's is often under diagnosed in adults over 30. They missed being screened as children or as females tend to better cover the social impacts. Because of this, it is common to have a large population that do not meet the formal criteria, but clearly display a wide range of the traits.

My "Cloud" concept of neurodiversity attempts to illustrate the degree and relative strength of a trait compared to others, not it's presence is the best measure. To the contrary having a large range of traits present even if minor is a good foundation for a well-rounded resilient person. It is when the number of condition related traits overshadow the rest of the personality traits that they shift their position in the neurodiversity cloud.

For a description of various scenarios that help to understand dealing with Asperger's and those with traits in that direction, see the addendum on how Asperger's/HFA shows up at work.

III RESOURCES

Books
These are some of the very helpful books I often recommend:

NeuroTribes: The Legacy of Autism and the Future of Neurodiversity by Steve Silberman

Nerdy, Shy, and Socially Inappropriate: A User Guide to an Asperger Life by Cynthia Kim

22 Things a Woman Must Know: If She Loves a Man With Asperger's Syndrome by Rudy Simone

Life With a Partner or Spouse With Asperger Syndrome: Going over the Edge? Practical Steps to Savings You and Your Relationship by Kathy J. Marshack

Managing With Asperger Syndrome: A Practical Guide For White Collar Professionals by Malcolm Johnson

The Autistic Brain: Helping Different Kinds of Minds Succeed by Temple Grandin, Richard Panek

Organizations and websites
Yes you could just Google this yourself, but here are a few I found helpful to start with.

https://www.TimGoldstein.com
https://www.aspergerstestsite.com
http://www.aane.org
https://www.autismspeaks.org
http://www.autism-society.org

ABOUT THE AUTHOR

Tim's biggest interest is creating a bridge between the neurodiverse technical worker, who likely has Asperger's Syndrome traits, and the vast majority of the world that would be considered neurotypical, meaning normal in the way they think, process, and view the world. His goal is to help companies better understand and support the Aspie leaning technical employees to reduce turnover, increase engagement, and generate greater innovation and productivity from this hard to find class of unique geeky technical knowledge worker.

Tim has pursued a number of successful and unsuccessful careers spanning over 40 years. His initial career was in the bicycle and sporting goods industry.

After numerous dead-end jobs, Tim started a computer and IT career as a Microsoft Certified Systems Engineer (MCSE). He transitioned to programming and settled into the specialty of database development and business intelligence. Tim led an IT team of 15 people before changing his employment strategy to contracting and consulting with a specialty in short term distressed projects. This has given Tim extensive experience interviewing and seeing tech / non-tech interactions in a range of setting.

Over the last few years, Tim learned that many of the skills and traits which allow him to excel as a developer and problem solver come from the condition Asperger's Syndrome, which he has. Working with a vast number of IT and Engineering departments and many of the people in these industry, Tim noticed many engineers, programmers, developers, infrastructure support people, scientists, accountants, and professors display a number of the traits associated with Asperger's Syndrome.

Tim has interviewed hiring managers, HR leaders, and recruiters to identify the major areas IT workers struggle with in interviews based on the perspective of the people they need to convince to get the job. He then integrated common geek style thinking with his vast experience in sales and communication to create a simple approach to allow any geek, nerd, engineer, or IT worker to be the strongest interviewee and have one of the greatest chances to win the job.

Tim has also started multiple businesses including A2Z Corp, a manufacturing company, which he founded and ran for 10 years. Tim designed, created, and produced multiple products which created a strong international brand.

Tim has studied storytelling and public speaking as a Master Presenter mentor under Roger Love, coaching as a Certified High Performance Coach, and body movement and speaking authentically from the best trainers in their fields. In additional he has learned the method and skills of written and video content creation, Facebook marketing, knowledge business strategies, online course creation, as well as various other technologies, tools, and techniques to run a high quality training, coaching, mentoring practice.

In addition to writing books, Tim does speaking, custom training, coaching and mentoring in diverse field that are tied together by their need to interact with the technically minded geeky personality. You can contact Tim through his site www.TimGoldstein.com

When he is not working, one of Tim's favorite sports is hiking the 14,000 ft peaks of Colorado in the winter. Besides great exercise, the entire journey from preparing, reaching the summit or not, and getting back down all teach important lessons required to succeed in any pursuit. Even his experience of having a search and rescue crew catch up with him at 3:30 am at 12,000 ft in the winter has become an illustration of the huge difference in mental processing styles.

Tim lives outside Denver Colorado with his lifelong companion and wife Karen. (www.KarenGoldstein.com)

Made in the USA
Lexington, KY
15 April 2017